CONTENTS

Salvation and the Free Life of the Spirit in the Orthodox Canonical Tradition

SALVATION AND THE FREE LIFE OF THE SPIRIT IN THE ORTHODOX CANONICAL TRADITION

As Professor Emeritus of Canon Law at Holy Cross Greek Orthodox School of Theology and consultant on canonical issues to the Greek Orthodox Archdiocese of North America and other North American jurisdictions, Dr. Lewis J. Patsavos is the most respected and experienced Orthodox canonist in the West. Esteemed by hierarchs, colleagues, and decades of students for his traditional, incisive, and yet warmly pastoral approach to the Holy Canons, Dr. Patsavos offers *Road to Emmaus* readers a rich and often surprising introduction to the canonical tradition of the Orthodox Church.

RTE: Dr. Patsavos, to most laymen, Orthodox canon law appears to be a compilation of centuries of rules that command or forbid various behaviors with rather strict penalties for not fulfilling them. Reading the collection of canons in *The Rudder* is daunting, and many of us find it difficult to reconcile them with the real circumstances of our lives. Knowing our own weakness, we are intimidated by what appears to be a severe and thorny legal tradition. However, as you point out in your Canon Law classes, this is not what the Fathers or the Councils had in mind, and for most students, your class

Opposite: Professor Lewis J. Patsavos.

is a revelation. In your introductory lecture you remarked, "For the earthly Church, canons constitute the external means of security within which the free life of the spirit is developed. Their ultimate purpose is man's salvation." That was a completely unexpected opening.

DR. PATSAVOS: I'm happy to hear this because, as a professor, I sometimes wonder what the students do hear. I feel this living quality of the canons passionately and it is so sad when people take them as dry texts to be adhered to as law. This is not at all what the Orthodox canons are, and rather than "canon law," I much prefer the term "canonical tradition" as a more genuine description of this great gift of the Holy Spirit. Due to a variety of circumstances, this gift is not well known, and anything that isn't well known is subject to distortion and misunderstanding.

The present confusion in our canonical thinking comes from not understanding that tradition cannot be fully reduced to legal categories. Those who affirm the legal absoluteness of all canons neglect the fact that the Church itself has forgotten or set aside some of these canons for centuries, while those who discount the tradition of the canons altogether are dismissing the Church itself.

Because of this danger of distortion and misunderstanding, I would caution anyone who is not educated in the canonical tradition from going to *The Rudder* (*Pedalion* in Greek), the most common of several traditional collections. If one doesn't know the history of *The Rudder*, who translated it, the problems with the existing (especially English) translations, and which commentaries have been added by the translator and editors that were not in the original text, they can find themselves with serious misunderstandings. No one should read *The Rudder* without a background in the history and practice of the Orthodox canonical tradition.

To understand the canons one needs to be educated in scripture, Church history, the role the Fathers play in the Church and their writings, and some knowledge of Greek. If you don't have these basics, you won't understand the content of the canons. Also, there are some very harsh things said in *The Rudder*—not necessarily in the canons themselves, but in the commentaries and interpretations of the canons that were added later. In the case of *The Rudder*, the interpreter-commentator was St. Nikodemos of the Holy Mountain, an eighteenth-century monk whom we revere as the patron saint of the science of canon law. At the same time, St. Nikodemos viewed the canons through the context and times in which he lived, and because of this his comments can appear harsh.

This outlook is not necessarily that of the Church Fathers who wrote the canons, nor of the councils which ratified them. While we venerate St. Nikodemos, we don't know if all of his interpretations accurately reflect the intent of the original authors. This does not lessen his sanctity, but the danger for someone reading *The Rudder* who is not familiar with the structure and tradition of canon law is that they won't understand the difference between a canon and its interpretation, and may think that the interpretation is as authoritative as the canon itself. It is not.

RTE: Can you briefly explain about the nature of canons and how they've come down to us?

DR. PATSAVOS: The word canon comes from the Greek word *kanon*, metaphorically, "a ruler," and further, something that makes a straight line. Thus, a canon is a teaching or a decision that has been given to assist us in our struggle to achieve spiritual perfection and salvation. Interestingly, it is from that image that the name "Rudder" was given to this collection of the canons. If you open to the beginning of *The Rudder*, you always see the picture of our Lord and His disciples in a boat, with the Lord at the helm steering the rudder. The rudder symbolizes this collection of canons that directs us towards the safe haven, to God's kingdom. The canons are enlivened by the presence of the Holy Spirit, who helps us understand their role in the Church. Just imagine what life would be like if we had no parameters.

RTE: Perhaps like driving without traffic rules.

DR. PATSAVOS: We can think of canons as guidelines but not as laws, because with laws we immediately conjure up images that are foreign to what the canons are. The canons are not meant to be laws like the laws of the state, and they are not enforced by coercion. If you commit yourself to the Orthodox Christian faith, then you willingly adopt the lifestyle and ethos expressed by the canons. They are clarifying teachings.

Dogmatic and Practical Canons

RTE: With such a great number and variety of canons—855 listed in *The Rudder*—are they are all of equal value?

DR. PATSAVOS: In the Orthodox tradition we have both dogmatic canons and practical canons. A dogmatic canon clarifies a doctrinal truth and these canons are considered universal and unalterable—*horoi* or *dogmata* in Greek—while more practical canons regulate the external life of the faithful through order and discipline. These can be changed to meet the needs of the Church. However, the Church doesn't distinguish one as more important than the other.

The dogmatic canons are vital because in the early Church there were many false teachings and it was important for the Church to clarify what is true Orthodox belief and what is false. These dogmatic canons are unalterable and cannot be changed. For instance, the canons that make reference to the Three Persons of the Holy Trinity as the basis for the triple immersion of baptism can never be altered. However, there can be changes in canons of order and discipline. For instance, one of the canons prohibits marriage with a non-Orthodox person, yet we know that today, under certain circumstances, the Church does bless marriage with non-Orthodox Christians. This is a matter of order and structure, not of dogma.

RTE: Times, people and situations change, and it brings to mind the Lord's words: "The Sabbath was made for man, not man for the Sabbath."

DR. PATSAVOS: Exactly, yet our responses cannot be arbitrary, there must be legitimate reasons for change. For instance, even today an Orthodox Christian may not marry any non-Orthodox Christian, but only those who themselves believe and have been baptized in the name of the Holy Trinity. Also, they must be married in an Orthodox Church.

However, these canons of order and discipline are not practiced uniformly in every Orthodox jurisdiction. I cannot speak authoritatively for them all, but where there is a predominantly Orthodox population, it is less likely that the local church would permit such marriages with non-Orthodox. Here in America, we have to be pastorally sensitive to the reality that we Orthodox are a small minority, and because of this, it is very difficult to uphold the strictness of this canon. Certainly, the ideal is to uphold the strictness, because nothing makes more sense than having a marriage of two people who are committed to the same belief, yet we also know from our experience that mixed marriages can be successful when the husband and wife are compatible and are themselves flexible.

RTE: I recently attended a Greek Orthodox marriage preparation seminar. Out of the thirteen couples, only two were Orthodox marrying Orthodox. I cannot imagine marrying someone with whom I would not be able to receive Holy Communion, but many Orthodox Christians seem not to feel this.

DR. PATSAVOS: Yes, this is a sad realization, but on the other hand, it has been pointed out that this is one way that people who would otherwise never experience Orthodoxy are led to the Orthodox Church—providing, of course, that the Orthodox spouse is committed to his or her faith. Many people come to Orthodoxy through marriage.

Approaches to Canon Law in the East and West

RTE: Dr. Patsavos, will you please describe the canonical sources and explain why, although we have these common roots, the Orthodox canonical tradition differs from Roman Catholic canon law?

DR. PATSAVOS: It's true that we have many common sources. Initially the canons came from scripture, from Holy Tradition, from documents issued by regional and ecumenical councils, and from early accepted writings, including *The Didache, The Apostolic Constitutions, The Tradition of Hippolytus,* and other anonymous codified works such as *The Shepherd of Hermas.* We don't know the authors, but these were attempts to record the practice of the Christian faith in the early Church. Although the early Church had no precise juridical organization, juridical elements are already present in the authority of these early writings.

In later centuries, when the Church was recognized officially by the state, we also have statements and edicts from Byzantine emperors that were incorporated into the canons. For example, the decision regarding the celibacy of bishops originated as state legislation, and afterwards the Church ratified it as a canon. So, Christianity in both East and West shares these common sources.

As centuries passed, the sources proliferated until you had such a vast number of canonical teachings that it was very difficult for those who were not educated in this discipline to discover the canonical position of the Church on a specific subject. To rectify this, the western Church eventually codified its collection of canonical sources, classifying them by subject. In the West, of course, certain characteristics of the Roman mind predominated, such as an emphasis on structure (I purposely want to stay away from terms like juridical or legalistic), whereas in the East you have more of a freethinking philosophical mind, a more abstract approach to theological definition.

RTE: When you speak of western codification, you mean that everything on marriage is in one section, on ordination in another, and so on?

DR. PATSAVOS: Yes, there are sections of canons on the sacraments, on the organization of the Church, on personal moral behavior. As a result, in the Roman Catholic Church you have an enormous and comprehensive collection that has explored the vast array of canonical sources on these subjects and, in addition, further defined them. Nothing has been left out. For any possible circumstance, a priest or bishop can go to the canons to find a precise response. This is the prescriptive approach to canon law, where not only are situations addressed that have actually arisen, as in the uncodified eastern canons, but every foreseeable circumstance has been anticipated and legislated upon.

This prescriptive codification doesn't exist in the eastern Christian approach. Here you simply have the same vast array of early canonical sources, listed by their authors or the councils that adopted them. These sources include the early writings I've already mentioned, along with the edicts of emperors, councils, and some writings of the Church fathers, including St. Basil the Great (from whom we have 92 canons), St. John Chrysostom, St. Peter of Alexandria, St. Nicephorus the Confessor, St. John the Faster, and St. Gregory the Theologian.

We may recognize some of these fathers as old friends, while others aren't as familiar, but they all addressed actual issues that the councils were grappling with. When the hierarchs of an ecumenical council found an answer to their question in the writings of one of those great fathers, they would quote it, saying, "This is written about in such and such a letter of St. Basil."

Needless to say, these saints did not sit down to write canons; we have their answers in treatises, sermons, and in letters where questions have been put to them. Saint Basil, for example, responded to specific questions and he also wrote treatises, such as his famous work on the Holy Trinity, and these were confirmed as authoritative at an ecumenical council.

So, the Church distilled these original lengthy answers and treatises of the Church fathers, the early canonical writings, the edicts of emperors and regional councils and so on, into canonical rules or regulations. These issues were often first brought up in provincial councils that met to discuss the practical issues surfacing in a diocese or province.

Canons of some of these provincial councils, such as Ancyra, Neocesarea, Gangra, Carthage, and so on, were later recognized by the highest human Church authority, an ecumenical council. In one of its canons, the Sixth Ecumenical Council mentions all of the recognized provincial or regional councils. Although there were many councils that made decisions, only a number were accepted as valid, authentic, and authoritative by the Sixth Ecumenical Council.

Another practical tool we have in the eastern churches are charters, and all of the Orthodox jurisdictions and local churches have their own constitution or charter. This is a legal document outlining how the local church is governed that always reflects the universal canons. For instance, the 34th Apostolic Canon decrees that the Church is governed by a council, not by a single bishop. While in the Roman Catholic Church the highest human authority is invested in the bishop of Rome, in the Orthodox Church the highest authority is not invested in the person of the patriarch of Constantinople or any other patriarch, but in councils of bishops.

So, returning to your question of how East and West differ in their approach, although we did not systematize the canons like the Roman Catholics, we have gathered them into collections divided by council, text, or individual Church father. We go to these canons and say, "Based on this decision from the Council of Ancyra, this is what we should do." So, there is more room here for flexibility than a detailed prescriptive codification would allow.

RTE: The image that comes to mind of the difference between the western codified tradition and the more flexible eastern one is that of an iron lung as opposed to a living lung that freely takes in oxygen and expels waste. The iron lung is rather more solid, predictable, and maintains life, but it may lack the ability to serve as part of an organic whole and to adapt to changing circumstance. Is that too strong of an assessment?

DR. PATSAVOS: No. In fact one particular characteristic that defines our understanding of the canonical tradition is the principle of individualization. (The Greek word is equally long, *exatomikefsis*.) You can go to the penitential canons and recite by rote what St. Basil the Great has said about how a person who has committed adultery should be penanced and how many years he should be deprived of Holy Communion, but St. Basil himself wrote at length about this individualized approach, particularly in regard to confession and spiritual healing. We also have canons that direct us to this individual approach towards each person's sin and how to assess it.

RTE: This approach would include things like a person's age and understanding, their circumstances, and their willingness to repent?

DR. PATSAVOS: Absolutely. First of all is their understanding of the seriousness of what they have done and true remorse. If this is present, then the penance should be lessened. This principle of flexibility is apparent throughout the Orthodox canonical tradition.

RTE: Then are Roman Catholics strictly bound by their systematized canonical code?

DR. PATSAVOS: In a codified system, the individualized approach wouldn't be as apparent, but I don't want to create an adversarial view of the West's codified law. That our western brothers and sisters recognize the need for a pastoral approach is evident in their documents and decrees which use a more pastorally sensitive language than the codified canons, but it is safe to say that individualization is not practiced to the degree that it is in the East, simply because the mind of an eastern Christian doesn't operate as the mind of a western Christian.

RTE: Westerners living in a country such as Greece, Russia, or in Eastern Europe are usually surprised to find that although laws exist, they aren't always applied as we would expect. There is a different view of law.

Opposite: Mosaic circa 1000 AD. Equal-to-the-Apostles Constantine the Great presents Constantinople as a tribute to enthroned Theotokos and Christ Child, Church of St. Sophia, Istanbul.

DR. PATSAVOS: Yes, this need for codification is not so deeply felt, although as our western colleagues rightly point out, the imperial legislation of the Byzantine emperors was a major inspiration for the western codification of canon law. There were great jurists among the emperors and legal scholars of the Eastern Roman Byzantine Empire, but not within the Church, which is why until now there are many Orthodox who believe that to proceed with our own codification would very much change the canonical sensitivities for which the eastern church is known.

Nevertheless, our lack of codification makes us vulnerable to the pitfalls of distortion and abuse. It is presupposed that the person who is reading and interpreting the canons is qualified, educated, and grounded.

RTE: And has a pure motive.

DR. PATSAVOS: Precisely. These presuppositions are essential to correctly interpret the canons. Interpretation also presupposes that the spirit of the teaching has been truly understood and encapsulated in the written canon. The drawback to this is that because the Church is within the world, and history is a part of life in the world, there is always change, so the canonical tradition itself needs periodic updating. Even western codification isn't static because, in time, it too will reach the predicament we are faced with in the East, where we are dealing with texts that go back to the third and fourth centuries. This cannot be easily corrected because only a synod of equal or greater importance than the one that promulgated the legislation can effect a change in a canon, usually an ecumenical council.

RTE: Dr. Patsavos, as we know, in the past few centuries, western theology has influenced Russian, Greek, and Balkan Orthodoxy. Do you think that the historical circumstances that prevented us from having ecumenical councils might have also kept us from going down the road of western codification and developing a more rational ethos? I'm speaking historically, of course, because we believe that the Holy Spirit is the great determiner in all of this.

DR. PATSAVOS: It is true that Orthodox theology was influenced by the West at a time of decline in theological thought and that theologians like Romanides, Florovsky, and others have helped us recover our past free from outside influences, but given the eastern mindset, I doubt whether we would have gone the course of the West even if circumstances had allowed.

We in the East, and the great fathers and mothers of the eastern Church, reflect an ethos that is immediately identifiable and different from the mindset of the West. One thing that comes to mind is scholasticism, particularly the Aristotelian theology of Thomas Aquinas. That exactitude is not evident in the writings of the Greek Fathers, and this is partly due to the Platonic philosophical training of the fathers of the East, whose more abstract mindset plays out in how the Orthodox address theological issues. Their theological precision has a more philosophical expression.

The East did not have the presuppositions necessary for codification, nor did they feel the need for codification. These kinds of things simply did not preoccupy the eastern mind. The reason codification is so frequently mentioned in our own day is because of the prevalence of this kind of thinking within canon law generally, particularly in the Roman Catholic Church and the Anglican Communion. We Orthodox are influenced by this because we all share the canonical sources of the early councils and we see the practical ramifications of not being more explicit. This western setting makes it difficult for Orthodox to practice our faith without more direction because we've conditioned ourselves accordingly.

In a pluralistic society we Orthodox find ourselves saturated with this western exactness, but going back to the term *exatomikefsis*, there is an openness to the individual circumstances of every situation. We do not say, "This is how this situation should be resolved. Make it a canon and enforce it in every applicable situation!" This is not an eastern approach.

However, because we live in a modern pluralistic society where everything is accessible and known, the abstract nature of the Orthodox ethos is going to be an easy target, one that is going to be misunderstood and abused. We are in a position where we can no longer be isolated. We have to begin to explain ourselves and how and why we diligently uphold the spirit of these holy canons, while taking into account individual circumstance.

RTE: Would we say then that the Holy Spirit inspires the letter of the canon, but it is also the Holy Spirit Who shows us how to apply the canon?

DR. PATSAVOS: Exactly.

Hagia Sophia Church, Site of First Ecumenical Council, Nicea (now Iznik, Turkey).

Canon Law and Canonical Tradition

RTE: Dr. Patsavos, you said earlier that you don't like the phrase "canon law" and prefer "canonical tradition". Will you explain why?

DR. PATSAVOS: Yes. The term "canon law" was adopted from the West just as we adopted other universally understood terms that assist us in dialog but which may not be quite our own. To use the word "law" immediately creates the impression that, "Here is another *system of law,*" while the term "canonical tradition" allows us to more easily project the understanding that this tradition is superior to any legal system. Just as the source of the Church is the divine will of God the Trinity, likewise, we believe that decisions reflected in the canons are the will of God for the governing of His Church on earth. That immediately puts it into a completely different category. When the source is God, then the goal or purpose is our salvation. On this subject Abp. Jerome Kotsonis says, "Since the holy canons constitute an expression of the Holy Spirit, Who lives within the Church, the only way to interpret them is by the Spirit." No system of law even comes close to this. No system of law claims a divine source or that its purpose is eternal salvation. That in itself sets it apart.

Now, why do some people confuse the Orthodox canons with a system of law? Externally, it has some similarities, but anyone with a legal background understands that they are not laws. First of all, they haven't been codified, and secondly, they are not understood in the same way that laws are: there is no coercion, there are no physical consequences. There are spiritual consequences if you do not follow them, but these you willingly accept if you wish to live according to the ethos of the Orthodox Church. There is an Orthodox life-style and this means you can't say, "I believe what the Orthodox Church teaches, but I'm going to live like a Protestant." There is a different *phronema*, a different ethos, a different understanding of discipline, asceticism and all the rest.

Something else that I touched on earlier is that our canons are not prescriptive. They never addressed a hypothetical situation, but only an event that *actually took place* and that was brought to the attention of the council where the issue was discussed. A decision was reached to either put a stop to this situation or to respond to it if it should arise again. Orthodox canon law does not conceive of a hypothetical scenario that might someday happen in order to give a pre-determined response. There are no prescriptive canons.

In fact, one must absolutely understand each canon's detailed historical context in order to grasp its spirit: What was going on? What was the early Church trying to address? How has the canon been applied through the centuries? Is the situation to which we are trying to apply this canon the same today?

RTE: This was underlined by a class assignment you gave, in which we each picked a single canon and researched the historical reasons for its adoption, how that particular canon has been interpreted throughout Church history, and how it might be applied in our own time while remaining true to its original intent and spirit. This was hard work, but it was clear that each canon has a life of its own, a history and application that we would never have anticipated. It was fascinating.

DR. PATSAVOS: I consider this exercise essential for understanding how canons should be interpreted; otherwise, one is tempted to interpret them literally. When they are interpreted literally it is almost always a misinterpretation. An answer in black or white is easier to follow, of course, than to reflect on the multi-faceted aspects of the canons, but a spiritually mature pastor should be able to adjust his approach accordingly.

Canonical Freedom and Creative Penances

RTE: I am particularly struck when you speak of canonical tradition, not as a "law" that has a hold over us, but as something that we voluntarily join ourselves to, a connection to the living Church that includes all of its members, past and present.

DR. PATSAVOS: Exactly, and speaking of the "hold" the canons have over us, they have no hold over us. They are not restrictive, they are freeing, and this is precisely what the Gospel is about. Christ did not come to impose another set of laws on us; He came to free us from the oppression of the misunderstanding of law.

When we abide by the spirit of what the canons say—for example, those that address our unhealthy compulsions and passions—we are freed from the hold that those distorted ways of being have over us. This is precisely what the disciplinary canons are about. Now, ill-advisedly, people read some of the canonical penances and interpret the word "penance" as punishment. I must emphasize that *penances are not punishments*, nor are they conditions of forgiveness. They are sanctions given to assist us in our effort to overcome whatever has imprisoned us.

RTE: Would a secular analogy of penance be the twelve steps of Alcoholics Anonymous, which says, "If you follow these steps consistently, honestly, and persistently, with God's help you will become sober." It is not a punishment, but the actual means by which you free yourself from bondage.

DR. PATSAVOS: Yes, and in a sense that is also a type of penance. Historically, one of the common penances imposed in the early Church was the deprivation of Holy Communion, which is called minor excommunication (there are degrees of excommunication). This word also frightens people, but a true understanding of minor excommunication is simply that someone is not yet ready to partake of Holy Communion.

In the early Church, Holy Communion was taken at every celebration of the liturgy and this was expected. After some centuries—and there were historical reasons for this—there were periods when Communion was received infrequently, and there are still many parishes in America where parishioners are scandalized if they see people going up week after week as they did in the early Church. We are trying to return to the early practice of more frequent Communion, which I applaud, but this does not mean that you go to a party on Saturday night to drink and dance and then receive Holy Communion on Sunday. The early Church presupposed a spiritual preparation of fasting, prayer and self-examination, and to tell someone not to take Communion for a year was devastating, but it helped them to understand the seriousness of their fall and that they had to exercise all of their strength to overcome that which was overcoming them.

It is a challenge to properly apply these canons, and sadly, in these times of infrequent communion, simply telling people that they can't take Holy Communion for a year may not affect them greatly. As a spiritual father, you need to find something constructive instead. If the failing is one of greed, make it a point for them to do a weekly charitable act, to seek out an organization or a family that needs support. If someone is addicted to rubbish on television, have them read religious literature or good classic novels. There is flexibility and room for creative penances in the canonical tradition of the Church.

The point is, what are you going to do to strengthen this person's spiritual growth? It is only through the grace of the Holy Spirit that the spiritual father is able to discern the real condition of the penitent and what will help.

RTE: Regarding confession, there seem to be two traditions—the Slavic practice of a brief, sometimes weekly confession before each Communion and the Greek practice of a much less frequent but more comprehensive confession that is not necessarily attached to Holy Communion.

DR. PATSAVOS: Yes, would that there was a happy medium, because neither of the two traditions is quite proper. The need for confession is always present, but there are sins that lead to death, and the much less serious sins of everyday life and habit. Because we are constantly sinning, these confessions of everyday matters are more like a dusting, which the Slavic churches are very conscientious about. However, one needs to make this distinction, because these less serious sins are not conditions that need to be confessed before every Communion.

RTE: You spoke earlier about spiritual freedom restoring the communion of love between God and humankind in Christ, which we activate by rejecting our fallen will. Can you enlarge on this?

DR. PATSAVOS: As human beings we need structure. We crave structure, just as a child who does not have a proper family craves it. He needs the consolation that the oversight of parents affords. In the same way, the canons are that consolation that there is something greater that guides us in our struggle. It is a human need that is being met.

What we have today is a misunderstanding of freedom that is reflected in the Greek word *asydosia*, meaning "no boundaries". This notion of boundless freedom is a misunderstanding of freedom, and from the Christian perspective, actually enslaves us. When we are committed to Jesus Christ, we are absolved of our slavery. For example, many people dismiss fasting in the 21st century as obsolete and belonging to the past, but we need fasting to harness that compulsion to break loose. For many of us this takes an entire lifetime and perhaps that is why our loving and forgiving Lord allows some of us a longer life than others. It takes us longer to get there.

Excommunication

RTE: You mentioned degrees of excommunication. Why and how would someone be excommunicated?

DR. PATSAVOS: The term excommunication means "out of communion". Excommunication can range from abstention from Holy Communion (self-imposed or imposed as penance) to expulsion from life within the Church altogether (*anathema*). An example of self-imposed excommunication is when one refrains from Holy Communion (today often for the wrong reasons). In the Early Church, excommunication could be imposed for a minor infraction such as absenting oneself from the liturgy for three Sundays in succession without a serious reason, or for a grave moral sin such as adultery.[1] The ultimate excommunication would have been expulsion from the worshipping community for spreading heresy. Depending upon the severity of the infringement, the length of excommunication could vary from days to years. Today, lengthy excommunication is rarely, if ever, imposed, except for a very grave sin such as heresy. This is done as much for the well-being

1 Lewis J. Patsavos, *A Noble Task: Entry into the Clergy in the First Five Centuries,* Holy Cross Orthodox Press, Brookline, MA, 2007.

Opposite: Seventeenth-century icon of the Seventh Ecumenical Council. Courtesy Novodevichy Convent, Moscow.

of the community as for the hoped-for repentance of the sinner. It is always imposed following the decision of a synod on the highest level.

RTE: I remember that in your book, *A Noble Task*, you have a marvelous quote by St. Ambrose of Milan on the virtue of almsgiving, who said that we need to take care, not only of the poor, but of the imprisoned, of captives taken as slaves, and even of those under serious canonical penance: "Though the faithful should benefit first, we cannot forget the excommunicated." How would we apply this today?

DR. PATSAVOS: We should think of it in terms of reaching out to everyone, even those with whom we are not in communion, including the non-Orthodox.

The Church's Ecclesiastical Conscience

RTE: Growing up in the West, most of us are so constrained by the straitjacket of rational, legalistic thought, that the idea of canons as "the will of God" is astonishing. How would Orthodox councils and hierarchs deal with a canon that seems not to be from God, but a mistake of fallen humanity?

DR. PATSAVOS: This is the place of ecclesiastical conscience in the Church. The ecclesiastical conscience is the common understanding of what is true and authentic. This consensus of the entire people of God, clergy and laity, presupposes the guidance of the Holy Spirit. If the people of God are in communion with the Holy Spirit, they understand what is authentic. If they are not, in time their decision will show itself as inauthentic.

RTE: Such as the "robber" and iconoclast councils?[2]

DR. PATSAVOS: Yes, and this communion with the Holy Spirit is something that cannot be measured. This is precisely what the West finds hard to deal with in our canonical tradition, because they can't put their finger on it.

---

2 The Second Council of Ephesus of 449 (commonly known as the Robber Council of Ephesus) was a church synod whose decrees were never accepted as ecumenical and were repudiated in 451 by the Fourth Ecumenical Council of Chalcedon. Likewise, the iconoclast Council of Hieria of 754 considered itself ecumenical in supporting the iconoclasm of Emperor Constantine V, but was overturned in both East and West by the Lateran Council of 769 and the Seventh Ecumenical Council (Second Council of Nicaea) in 787, which supported the veneration of icons.

When this subject of inauthentic decisions comes up in our Orthodox-Catholic discussions I often say, "Sometimes it will take years, but sooner or later the truth will prevail." They smile and reply, "That's the problem with you Orthodox, you are up in the clouds, you are not down-to-earth," and we answer, "And that's what's the matter with you, you are too confined to the earth." (*laughter*)

RTE: Then, if human mistakes can be made in promulgating canons and later be corrected, how can we say that canons are the fruit of the Holy Spirit?

DR. PATSAVOS: The distinction between dogmas and canons is that dogmas are absolute truths and canons are applications of these truths for the historical existence of the Church. Canonical decrees are only canonical when they serve as an expression of a dogmatic teaching. Thus, if a new decision genuinely reflects the Church, then the underlying dogmatic teaching for both the new and old canons remains unchanged: "The temporal as an expression of the eternal, the alterable as an expression of the unalterable."

Further, the true understanding of Holy Tradition is not a mechanical repetition of the past but the uninterrupted flow of life and creativity in the undiminishing grace that abides in the Church. If, during periods of decline, the organs of the Church's authority inadequately follow the Church's reality, then living Tradition will make up for this deficiency—this is when customs arise. No matter how serious the distortions of mistaken canonical decrees, they are not capable of suppressing the Church's life in grace. Errors in canon law are usually a result of a *decline in creativity*, an extinguishing of the Spirit. If there are errors, they are errors of man's will and eventually they will be rectified.

Facing New Situations

RTE: If universal canons can only be ratified in ecumenical or all-Church councils, how do we face new situations?

DR. PATSAVOS: The last ecumenical council was in the eighth century. What happened after that? Well, we've reached the twenty-first century and the Church is still functioning and still making decisions. Many of these decisions were reached regionally, not by universal consensus, and this is why we don't have a common approach on some issues. On the status of sacraments outside the Orthodox Church, for instance, we currently have a fairly common approach, but there were centuries when there was a variety of practices. Nevertheless, there were always ecclesiastical bodies that made decisions for the Church, and after the last ecumenical council there were other types of councils.

For example, in the Patriarchate of Constantinople, patriarchal councils function as the highest level of ecclesiastical authority. The decisions that they make do not have the same authority as canons made by ecumenical councils but they have allowed the Church to function. Over the centuries they have decided on important contemporary issues, such as, "How do we respond to the Reformation?" These kinds of councils also play a significant role in difficult periods, such as when the churches of the Near East and Eastern Europe were under Ottoman domination. In those centuries, when larger councils were not allowed for political reasons, or were logistically difficult, these local councils were convened with the participation of the Patriarchates of Antioch, Alexandria and Jerusalem. There is a great deal of authority residing with the patriarchates, which is why, in nonessential matters, local churches can make decisions as long as they do not conflict with the pre-existing rulings of the Seven Ecumenical Councils. Tradition and custom may also take the place of missing canons, but custom wrongly used can lead to the misinterpretation of canons.

RTE: The Orthodox Great and Holy Council has been in preparation for decades. When it comes about, will the Orthodox consider this to be an Eighth Ecumenical Council? Do you feel that this council is needed, and if so, what do you hope to see come out of it?

DR. PATSAVOS: This upcoming council will not define doctrine because unlike the period of the Seven Ecumenical Councils, Christianity is now divided between East and West; nevertheless, it is very much needed to confront situations unique to the Church today. In view of the fact that communication has made the world accessible in all its vastness, one need only consider the capacity offered for progress or stagnation. To remain inactive is to invite a deterioration of whatever strengths we may have as a federation of self-governing churches. To actively engage in interaction is certain to promote benefits for the Orthodox Church as a whole.

Canons, Tradition, and Customs

RTE: Dr. Patsavos, you mentioned tradition and customs. Certainly, we have some very enduring customs in Orthodoxy. Do they ever attain canonical status?

DR. PATSAVOS: First, we need to distinguish customs from tradition. Tradition with a capital T is the continual practice or commitment to an understanding *based on written sources.* It is a steady ongoing practice that does not conflict in any way with a teaching ratified by an ecumenical council. Some of these written sources may include those revered early Church writings, like *The Apostolic Constitutions*, or *The Apostolic Tradition of Hippolytus*, or *The Didache*, where you find instructions on the lifestyle of the clergy or how the early Church practiced its ascetic discipline. They may not have been ratified by ecumenical councils, but if they reflect the living written practice of the early Church and have continued through the centuries, this is Holy Tradition.

A custom, on the other hand, is a practice that is usually identified with a local church. We have more local than universal customs and these local customs are not as ancient as Holy Tradition. They are later developments

Sixth-century Syrian Gold Marriage Belt with inscription: "From God Concord, Grace, Health." Courtesy Dumbarton Oaks Collection, Washington, D.C.

that may either come out of tradition or simply from force of habit. The 39th Canon of the Penthekte (Fifth-Sixth) Ecumenical Council says that local churches can have their own special "customs in each Church". If customs reflect a doctrinal truth, they can be followed, but to insist upon them or to elevate them to the status of an ancient canon or Holy Tradition is wrong. An example of a custom are some of the impediments to marriage. We have a whole list of different types of relationships that are impediments.

RTE: Isn't it usually to the fifth degree of relationship?

DR. PATSAVOS: Exactly. Which doesn't make sense to us today. It did make sense in the Byzantine era when families lived in smaller societies and everyone was related. These degrees of impediments were a figurative way of saying that to be too closely related, whether through blood or through a marital relationship, is not healthy. For instance, to have a member of your family marry a member of your spouse's family isn't good for a stable marriage.

RTE: As in two brothers marrying two sisters?

DR. PATSAVOS: Yes, and there have been a whole series of prohibited marriages based on these practices. This is why, in individual cases, the Church can free one from abiding by these impediments.

RTE: Then marriage impediments are customs?

DR. PATSAVOS: Generally speaking, that's right—unless an impediment is mentioned in the canons, and the very closest ones are. For instance, Canon 54 of the Penthekte Council prohibits the male sponsor, the godfather of a child, from marrying the child's widowed mother. This canon can never be dispensed with because this was ratified by an ecumenical council. However, to speak of offspring or other relatives of the sponsor not marrying relatives of the mother is to speak of customs that go beyond the initial canon. There are also other practices that do not relate to doctrinal truths and have no useful purpose. These prohibitions do not need to be upheld.

However, I warn my students that if the change of a custom is going to cause a scandal in a parish, you'd better be very careful about doing so. You don't just come in and change longstanding practices. It has to be done by degrees. People must be educated and gradually brought into an understanding of why the practice was introduced, and why today it might not be as useful.

This is the case with many liturgical practices—sometimes people will see a priest doing something a little differently than his predecessor did and think that it is wrong. I know, for example, that the Russians are very faithful to liturgical rubrics, which are much more plentiful in the Slavic tradition than in the Byzantine—such as the practice of closing the Royal Doors and the curtain during liturgy, whereas the Greeks usually leave the doors open, making the liturgy visible. These were customs related to iconoclasm, but when you raise these customs to details that make a sacrament "valid" or "invalid," it becomes nonsense.

RTE: I imagine that when different nations and peoples converted to Christianity, their desire to be faithful to this new ethos sometimes led them to enshrine custom. This is still a tendency of new converts. Without the experience to discern between Holy Tradition and local custom, they can embrace both indiscriminately. It might be easier if they just lived watchfully for a few years.

DR. PATSAVOS: That is precisely when people get into trouble over custom. Custom covers an array of things—even the dress of the clergy. For instance, some clergy are so attached to wearing the *kalimavkion* [a priest's hat] as if it were a sacred vestment that it has become an object of conflict.

RTE: Our liturgics professor clarifies this by saying: "It's not sacred, it's just a hat. It protects your head."

DR. PATSAVOS: Good for him. And we have to ask, "Is this what we are reducing Orthodoxy to—a piece of apparel that has been made into a mitre?" This is precisely one of those issues where one fails to understand what custom is. If a custom relates to a doctrinal truth, fine, but if it creates issues that cloud the doctrine or no longer serve its original purpose, then it needs to be changed.

RTE: May I bring up another example here? I've been told that there are canons stating that we must fast, but there are no canons describing exactly how we fast. The tradition of the strict fast—no oil, wine, fish, meat or dairy—helps us to stay within bounds and it's good to be obedient to a common practice, yet difficulties do arise, such as when the Russian missionaries came to Alaska and there were no grains, beans and very little fruit or vegetables. Our common fasting rules were instituted around the Mediterranean, not in the far North. Because they couldn't alter the diet, missionaries simply asked the Alaskan Christians to cut down on the amount they ate.

DR. PATSAVOS: That is precisely what *economia* is, variation from the norm. As you said correctly, the canons presuppose that those who fast know how to fast, but the canons themselves only speak of "dry food," which is food without oil (although, certainly, it can be boiled).

Generally speaking, the canons do not prescribe what should be; that is assumed. Instead, they usually correct what is not done properly. With regard to fasting, the canons do not prescribe the foods from which one should abstain, since that was a living practice. One would never eat meat intuitively, for instance, if one were fasting. Dairy products are considered in the same way, since they come from meat. The canons mention "dry food" as a replacement for one's usual diet. Also, they instruct when and for how long one ought to fast.

If you are going by the letter of the canons, this "dry food" is the "strict" fast, and there are people who fast without oil for the forty days of the Great Fast and also in Holy Week. The question is, how many people are able to fast like that, and what are the alternatives? Again, here we have the ability of the Church to adjust when the goal cannot be met. The spirit of these fasting canons is not that one conforms literally to dry food, but that one deprives oneself of certain foods. And here is where tradition comes in, where the two overlap. The canons speak of dry food, but tradition shows us that we refrain from meat and dairy and supplement this fast by including other foods—such as shellfish, fruit, and so on.

The tradition of the Church foresaw a much stricter practice than we see today, yet we also know that contemporary people aren't always going to be able to live up to these restrictions. These realities of our day—the different climates, availability and quality of food, different ages and conditions of people—were all considered when this issue was discussed by those planning for our upcoming Great and Holy Council. They recognized that there must be fasting, but that fasting should conform to the realities of each locality. This is not to impede the deep piety or enthusiasm of those who want to fast strictly, but such enthusiasm must not be imposed upon others who are less able to take that on.

RTE: Regional fasting guidelines, of course, would imply an obligation, but it would be sad to see a relaxation interpreted as permission to use one's own discretion. Setting our own standards is somehow artificial. Like making up your own prayer rule, it's hard to take it seriously. A friend once said, "I need to have the Church's bar set high—otherwise it just isn't worth the effort," and Orthodox abroad have said that they wouldn't change these fasting practices even if allowed because they like feeling linked to the Christians of the past, who also followed them. People experience real joy in coming together at Pascha to break the fast, but if we fast more according to our own inclinations, perhaps we lose both the communal struggle and a deep part of the celebration.

Opposite: "Syntagma of Canons," Codex of Matthew Vlastares. Courtesy Vatopedi Monastery, Mount Athos.

DR. PATSAVOS: Well put. I think the Fathers understood these things much better than some of us do today. The Fathers don't justify why they take these stances. They speak in the language of the time, and sometimes they are very brief in their responses—just responding to the issue without explaining why. We have to presuppose that there is a deep spiritual and psychological rationale that they understood.

Interpreting the Canons

RTE: The Russian theologian Nicholas Afanasiev has a beautiful phrase that you passed on to us: "Holy Canons are temporal expressions of eternal truths." We know, however, that historical conditions do change, so how do we look at canons that seem irrelevant or do not adequately address contemporary needs without being disrespectful of the movement of the Holy Spirit that first inspired them?

DR. PATSAVOS: Canons are the application of eternal truths to the historical existence of the Church. The truth these canons express is absolute. However, as I said earlier, the content of these canons *is not this truth itself, but the means by which it is expressed in a given historical moment.* That means they can change if necessary.

Proper change involves caution and discernment without embracing extremes. On the one hand we cannot call for new canons contrary in spirit to earlier canons. Radically new canons cannot transform the contemporary world, because here the world is transforming the Church. Nor, on the other hand, should we call for the preservation of the letter of the law in the face of contemporary pastoral need. With rigid insistence on retaining every old historic form regardless of new needs, the Church cannot transform the contemporary world. The Church cannot live only by existing canon law; it is impossible to avoid creative work.

RTE: What are the particular dangers or challenges of renewal in our time?

DR. PATSAVOS: The element of the need for historical change should not be overstressed; we should not let a necessary change in a canon be used as an excuse to alter its dogmatic content. Adapting the canons to today's needs must not be at the expense of the moral demands of the Gospel or the ascetic ethos of Orthodoxy because a humanistic approach deprives the Church of her own approach. Also, as I said earlier, only a synod of equal or greater importance than the one that promulgated the legislation can effect a change in a canon, usually an ecumenical council.

RTE: Would our contemporary questions about bioethics and the new reproductive technologies be an example of a need to develop new canons to uphold the sanctity of life in this modern context?

DR. PATSAVOS: In theory, yes. In the meantime, we have other sources, like the writings of the fathers, ecclesiastical statements or *ad hoc* synodal decisions from which to glean an Orthodox perspective on these matters. I also must say that even if a canon is historically circumscribed, the spirit of the canon and its directives are very applicable today. For instance, canons about reconciliation to the Church after apostasy during the early Christian centuries of persecution do not allude to our own day, but it is not difficult to imagine similar circumstances. From the instructions given by these canons, we see that we are accountable for our decisions.

RTE: Can you give us examples of canons that have been ignored for centuries because they are no longer applicable or because our historical circumstances have altered?

DR. PATSAVOS: This would include canons that refer to offices or practices of a bygone era such as doorkeepers, deaconesses, exorcists, and so on, as well as pagan practices that are no longer applicable. Also, canons for practices like absenting oneself from attending liturgy for three Sundays in succession, or leaving the liturgy after the reading of the Gospel are not applied as they were originally but are didactic reminders of one's obligations. Although not strictly enforced, these latter canons serve as a reminder of the goal toward which one should aspire.

As for examples of canons that are no longer applicable, one canon forbids the presence of clergy and even lay Christians at wedding celebrations, because some pagan celebrations were downright immoral. Another canon that proscribes "leaping" does not sound problematic in English, but we have to look at what the Greek word means. In this case the Greek word means lewd or suggestive dancing, which, of course, is what went on at pagan celebrations. Another example is the prohibition for actresses to marry prospective candidates for the priesthood. In the early Christian centuries, an actress was expected to do immoral things. This may not correspond exactly to reality today today, but on the other hand it is not difficult to imagine similar kinds of situations. Even in these obsolete canons, we have the decision of the early Church as a starting point for how the Church might respond today, though we rarely apply them with the same austerity.

On two occasions I've been asked about the prospective spouses of two of our seminarians. These young women were both opera singers. In this case, the early canons about actresses were concerned with pornography and licentiousness, and you cannot equate that extreme life-style with today's opera singers. On the other hand, from a pastoral perspective, it might be problematic if a parish felt that their presbytera's profession did not fit their idea of what a priest's wife should be doing, although generally people are now much more accepting of different professions. Nevertheless, all of these dimensions need to be considered.

RTE: I appreciate your touching on the necessity for canonists to know the Byzantine Greek used by the Fathers and the Councils. Even with the best possible translations, there may not be exact equivalents, such as your example of "leaping."

DR. PATSAVOS: Exactly. This is the problem with translation and why we discourage untrained Orthodox from reading *The Rudder*.

Akrivea and Economia

RTE: A few moments ago you mentioned the term *economia*. We laypeople hear much about economia, which is often referred to light-heartedly to explain the relaxation of a canon, or of a practice such as fasting, but we hear little about its opposite, *akrivea*, the exact fulfillment of a canon. What are economia and akrivea, really, and how do they work pastorally?

DR. PATSAVOS: Canon 102 of the Sixth Ecumenical Council states: "The character of a sin must be considered from all points and conversion expected. And so let mercy be meted out." We look at the maturity and circumstances of the person. Economia may be given, but strictness can also be a way to awaken them to the gravity of their sin. Saint Basil the Great says that nothing prescribed and institutionalized has such an objective value that the strict letter of exactness must be observed every time, and never the loving

Fresco of the First Council of Constantinople, 381. Courtesy Stavropoleos Monastery, Bucharest, Romania.

attitude of economy. Although we must individualize every situation, econo-mia as general leniency is a distortion. Neither is economia a juridical dis-pensation, but if one insists on seeing it as a dispensation, it is granted only for that specific instance. It does not set a precedent.

In Greek, the term economia also denotes the mode of existence of the one Godhead in Trinity through mutual indwelling, so it is theologically a much richer term than any thought of expediency or leniency. Economia may be considered as completing what is lacking, and through grace perfecting that which is not performed according to akrivea, the exact fulfillment of the canon. Economia does not abolish exactness because, through her love and grace, the Church makes up all that is lacking.

So, economia is commitment to the salvation of the individual, not a vio-lation, and condescension is extended not only to the living but to the dead as well. When we speak about the Church's condescension—its willingness to depart from the norm in its desire to bring all to salvation—we recognize that the status of the departed really lies in God's hands and that the earthly Church is not going to judge or define what has happened to this person's soul. For instance, the funeral service is commonly performed today for one who has taken one's own life. This is an act of economia, because it is not the Church that is going to determine if that person did or did not violate God's law. That will be determined by God.

RTE: Isn't it often assumed that the person who took his own life is mentally ill, with a judgement so impaired that he is not culpable?

DR. PATSAVOS: Yes, there may be circumstances that we in our human imperfection are unable to comprehend. For instance, we continually discover organic and genetic causes for the malfunction of the human body and mind. Who knows what will be discovered in the future? We cannot pass judgement on what drives a person to take his own life.

RTE: In Russia the Church does not do funeral services for those who commit suicide unless they were quite clearly mentally ill, but good pastors will not only deeply console the family and friends, but also encourage them to read the psalter, to pray privately, and to commend the person to God's mercy. Although they don't serve the funeral, that merciful spirit is the same.

DR. PATSAVOS: And let me be clear that it is not the official position of the Greek Church to perform the funeral in every instance, but it is more or less the popular practice. The official position would be the same as what you have just articulated for the Russian Church.

Nevertheless, the Church's mercy extends even to those who have departed this life. An example of this is in regard to theologians whose writings were anathematized after their death. This includes Origen (who would have been one of the greatest saints of our Church if some of his works had not been declared heretical) but who wrote at a time when theology was still nascent. There was no council in his lifetime to examine his works, and we do not condemn him as a person, even on the Sunday of Orthodoxy. Again, you see the attitude of the Church here: to spare the reputation of the individual whose life was otherwise God-inspired and to trust in God's mercy.

Giving Canonical Opinions

RTE: One of the most difficult services of the Church must be that of a canonist who advises hierarchs on how to apply canons in critical and unusual situations. A priest who worked in the offices of the Russian Orthodox Church told me of an instance where two Orthodox orphans from different parts of Siberia met at a summer camp, fell in love, and were married with four children before they finally learned that they were natural brother and sister. I never learned the decision in this case, but such tragic and complicated situations must take a great deal of wisdom to settle. Can you tell us generally what criteria you use in applying canons in difficult cases?

DR. PATSAVOS: One must always seek guidance in prayer, understanding that the ultimate authority in all matters is God Himself. The most a canonist can do in a situation like the one you cite is to provide a pastoral directive, leaving all else to God's mercy.

The Gift of Discernment

RTE: Dr. Patsavos, you make a compelling statement on pastoral care in the canon law manual used by the Holy Cross seminarians:

> The pastor who lives and understands the spirit of our tradition, an integral part of which are the holy canons, senses with the guidance of the Holy Spirit how to apply them correctly. This is the spiritual gift of discernment, which the Church fathers call *diakrisis*. The difficulty lies not in the fact that the canons are an anachronism but that we are unable to live according to their spirit. Every attempt to change the canons arbitrarily on the part of pastors and theologians who do not live the tradition is destined to fail. That which is urgently needed is what the fathers call *kale alloiosis*—the proper change of the pastor in the light of tradition.

Seeing how much background is needed to correctly interpret the canons, laypeople may sometimes wonder how they can realistically expect their parish priest or even their hierarch to negotiate this complex, rich, and venerable canonical tradition. People are understandably anxious about how these interpretations will affect their lives, and even with the best of inten-

tions, our clergy are rarely trained as canonists. How would you go about setting people's minds at ease?

DR. PATSAVOS: One must have deep faith, yet at the same time be solidly grounded in realistic expectations. The gift of *diakrisis* is not automatic and this is why one must diligently seek out spiritual fathers whose pious deeds reflect its possession. With spiritual maturity comes the ability to sense the presence of *diakrisis* in a spiritual father. Until then, one's constant prayer should be the attainment of such spiritual maturity and trust in God's intervention.

I would add here that there are parish priests who may not have *diakrisis*. They have been ordained to perform the sacraments for the spiritual sustenance of Orthodox Christians, and they may be good but rather worldly people. This is not to cast judgement on anyone because it is very difficult in our times to be without a degree of worldliness. Given that reality, there are also parishioners who are satisfied with a casual relationship with the Church and do not desire the loving prodding of a good spiritual father. You also have clergy who themselves are not fully developed spiritually and are unable to bring their spiritual children up to a higher level. It is only when a priest is engaged in spiritual growth and shows through his own example what it is to lead the Christian life that the Church's teaching becomes more than theory. If it is only theory, no one is going to follow.

It is difficult and challenging for people who hunger for more than they can receive in their parish. In desperation they go to places where they may be fed, but it may not be the right food.

RTE: Too much meat before they are ready?

DR. PATSAVOS: Either that, or the wrong meat, as they receive at some extreme monasteries, or from extreme monks in an otherwise spirit-filled monastery. This temptation exists because these people aren't being fed in their parishes. One of our biggest challenges is how to protect them from these dangerous situations.

RTE: You have remarked several times on differences between the Christian East and West. As American or European Orthodox Christian converts are

Opposite: Modern icon, The First Holy Ecumenical Council in Nicea. Provenance unknown.

generally raised in the Judeo-Christian West, do you feel that we can ever truly take on the Orthodox ethos?

DR. PATSAVOS: What is impossible with human beings is possible with God. It is true that the secular society of which we are a part in a sense predisposes us to see things very differently from the way the Church sees them. However, here again, one must be humble enough and honest enough to acknowledge the need to grow into the faith by degrees, to full maturity in time.

RTE: To end our very fruitful discussion, do you have any final thoughts?

DR. PATSAVOS: From a personal perspective, I believe that I have been blessed beyond measure as a layperson entrusted with such a weighty responsibility. This shows the strength of the Orthodox Church—that it can and does entrust the laity with something as important as the teaching of canon law. Although there may not be as many examples of women who have been entrusted with teaching, this too is beginning. The important thing here is that the lay element has not *come into* its own, it is at its own, and the Church continues to honor that tradition.

Secondly, I thank God because there is a growing appreciation of the holy canons. I have been a canonist for close to forty years and I am encouraged that we now have a whole generation of clergy and lay people who have heard about this neglected area of theological discipline. I hope and pray that there are budding canonists out there who will take on this mission to further the appreciation, study, and understanding of the canonical tradition of the Orthodox Church. This is the spirit with which I want to end my reflection. ✙

Dr. Lewis J. Patsavos, Professor Emeritus of Canon Law, taught at Holy Cross Greek Orthodox School of Theology for more than four decades, and continues to serve as Consultant on Canonical Affairs to the Greek Orthodox Archdiocese and other Orthodox jurisdictions in America. His book: *A Noble Task: Entry into the Clergy of the First Five Centuries* (Holy Cross Orthodox Press, 2008) details the canons and patristic texts relating to the priesthood and the praxis of ministry in the early Church.

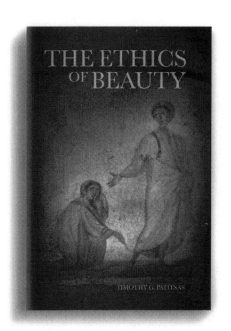

THE ETHICS
OF BEAUTY

TIMOTHY G. PATITSAS

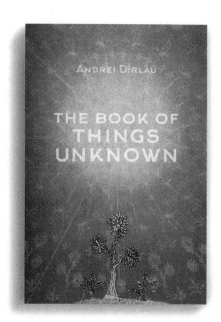

ANDREI DÎRLĂU

THE BOOK OF
THINGS
UNKNOWN

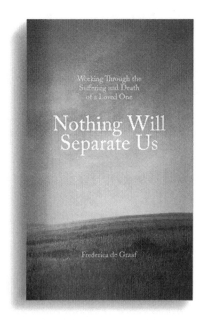

Working Through the
Suffering and Death
of a Loved One

Nothing Will
Separate Us

Frederica de Graaf

BRIGHT FAITH

*Father Artemy Vladimirov Talks
with Western Orthodox Christians*

A decade of collected interviews and articles from
Road to Emmaus: A Journal of Orthodox Faith and Culture

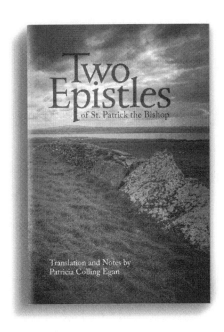

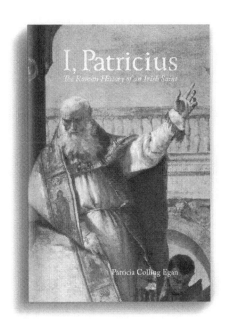

St. Nicholas Press

www.stnicholaspress.net

Made in the USA
Middletown, DE
26 September 2021

49155569R00029